nothin'BUT puffins

and other silly observations

Nancy McGinnis

nothin'
BUT puffins

and other silly observations

John McDonald

Down East

Front cover photo by Thomas O'Neil
Back cover photo by Nancy McGinnis
Design by Lynda Chilton

978-0-89272-547-2

Down East
BOOKS·MAGAZINE·ONLINE
www.downeast.com
Distributed to the trade by
National Book Network

Printed in China

5   4   3   2

Library of Congress Cataloging-in-Publication Data

McDonald, John.
  Nothin' but puffins / [captions] by John McDonald.
    p. cm.
  ISBN 978-0-89272-547-2 (alk. paper)
  1. Puffins--Humor. 2. Puffins--Pictorial works. I. Title. II. Title:
Nothing but puffins.
  PN6231.P795M36 2010
  818'.602--dc22

                    2010021436

For
Alison

The Power of the Puffin

When DOWN EAST asked if I would like to work on a puffin project, I agreed without hesitation. First, because I've always liked puffins (who doesn't?); and second, I thought, at my age, how many more puffin projects are likely to come over the transom here at Storyteller Central?

The project was to publish the book you're holding—a book of beautiful puffin photographs. My job was to write captions for each picture.

Soon after signing on I received my first group of puffin pictures. As my neighbor back home would say: "Ain't they cunnin'? " Yes, they are. Here were beautiful color images of puffins going about their puffin lives: landing and taking off from ocean-bound granite piles, seeming to have serious conversations with each other while precariously standing on slanted, jagged out-cropping, and my favorite—a contented puffin, strutting purposefully along, a beak full of eels and squid, looking like he just left an all-you-can-eat seafood buffet.

As a kid I remember the first time I saw puffins up close. It was the summer my father bought what became his pride and joy—a thirty-eight-foot, Stonington-built, cedar-on-oak lobsterboat. With it we were able to go out into the Gulf of Maine and cruise by the ledges where puffins hung out in great numbers.

With binoculars we took turns watching as these lovable birds went

Nancy McGinnis

"So I say, 'Doc, it hurts when I do this.' And he says, "Well, don't do that. That'll be fifty bucks.""

about their daily lives—just like they're doing in these photographs. When I saw the current pictures they brought back fond memories of those first encounters with puffins. Just like now, those puffins were just sitting and relaxing, swaggering from one place to another or standing and looking out at us as we glided by in our boat.

Over the last few months I've learned more about puffins than I knew back then. For example, did you know that puffins spend most of their lives at sea and only come ashore on remote islands to carry on their courtship, breed, lay their eggs, and hatch their chicks? Once that important business is completed, it's back out to sea.

As to who should buy this book? A good question, and one I've given a lot of serious thought to. I'd say anyone who owns a coffee table should buy this book without hesitation. Not only will it be ready to entertain your guests, but, because of its size, it can share your coffee table comfortably with your other coffee-table books.

If you like seabirds, or you're a maritime person, or you'd eventually like to join either of those groups, you should also buy this book for your collection. Come to think of it, I can't think of anyone who wouldn't want this book for their collection.

Knowing everyone is a critic, I'd be curious to know what you think.

John McDonald
Otisfield, Maine

"*No birdwatchers on this side.*
How about on your side?"

I swear Red's Eats was around here somewhere.

Thomas O'Neil

"He went that way."

Thomas O'Neil

Nancy McGinnis

"Well, it's obvious you haven't been brushing and flossing regularly, but other than that, your mouth looks fine."

"*Marco*"

*"You had me at
'sardine.'"*

"Polo"

"How many puffins
does it take to screw
in a lightbulb?"

Thomas O'Neil

"What's a lightbulb?"

Thomas O'Neil

"I always knew
that group was
stuck up."

"Yes? Question in the second row?"

Erik Christensen

"*I like my sushi still wiggling.*"

"Puffin love: a many splendored thing."

"That take-off looked good..."

Thomas O'Neil

Thomas O'Neil

"...but, oh, the judges will definitely deduct points for that."

Thomas O'Neil

"There's got to be a better place than this to lay my eggs, but where?"

Thomas O'Neil

"Hey, where'd everybody go? Come back!"

"Talk about being stuck between a rock and a hard place!"

Puffin bling

Thomas O'Neil

"No, you shut up!"

"No, you shut up!"

Steve Deger

"I'm not backin' off, you back off!"

"Shhhh! Don't let that photographer know we're up here."

Nancy McGinnis

"*Well, it's not as good as regular dental floss.*"

Thomas O'Neil   Thomas O'Neil

"Hear Ye! Hear Ye!"

"This must be the Hard Rock Cafe."

Thomas O'Neil

Jörg Hempel

"Who knew that last helping of fish would make it so hard to take off?"

"Do these tail feathers
make me look fat?"

*"I could go for a quarter flounder
with cheese right now."*

"There's no way the girls down there aren't impressed with this."

There once was a puffin from Popham...

"I said: 'BLG BDMR
NUDMBF!'"

Thomas O'Neil

"You want a piece of this?"

Nancy McGinnis

"What? You're going to ignore me, just because
I don't have a fancy orange beak like yours."

"Check this out...echo!"

Nancy McGinnis

ECHO!

ECHO!

"Whoa…
that's wicked
awesome."

Nancy McGinnis

41

"Flaps down, cleared for final approach."

Nancy McGinnis

"I don't care what that photographer says, this is definitely my best side."

"What do you mean, 'No room?'
I see plenty of room."

"Don't hate me because I'm beautiful."

"Puffins to the left of me, puffins to the right...I really need a break from this place."

"You never take me anywhere anymore."

Nancy McGinnis

Nancy McGinnis

46

"Oh, they hear
you all right—
they're just
ignoring you."

Nancy McGinnis

Thomas O'Neil

"*Everybody tells me how cute I am, but, to be honest, I'm not feeling it right now.*"

And the medalists are...

Thomas O'Neil

Nancy McGinnis

"Yes, your breath does smell fishy."

Rock star.

Nancy McGinnis

"Wow! *That plant food really works.*"

Nancy McGinnis

Nancy McGinnis

"I swear that sardine was this big if he was an inch."

Thomas O'Neil

"I know I left those keys somewhere."

Nancy McGinnis

"Guys, do you think Jim's okay?
He's been up there
a long time."

"'What's for lunch?' Are you kidding! What do you think's for lunch, Einstein? What's ever for lunch around here? FISH! That's what's for lunch."

"Eeewwww, I think I just
stepped in something."

"Can't we find a flatter place to hold these meetings?"

"And I thought the summit at Katahdin was crowded."

Nancy McGinnis

Nancy McGinnis

"You can come out now, the cruise boat is gone."

"Shhh! Your mother is trying to sleep!"

"There goes Hotwings, showing off again."

Nancy Mc

"You must be this tall to enter. No exceptions."